BLACKS IN OHIO

7 PORTRAITS

Edited by John A. McCluskey
Assistant Professor of English
Case Western Reserve University

THE NEW DAY PRESS
KARAMU HOUSE
Cleveland, Ohio

ACKNOWLEDGEMENTS

This publication was in part made possible
by financial assistance from the following:

The Ohio Arts Council
A. H. S. Foundation
N. L. Dauby Charity Fund

It bears the endorsement of the Greater
Cleveland Bicentennial Committee

Contributors' photographs are courtesy of
Hugh L. Gaines. Martha Lee Smith served
as editorial/graphics coordinator.

ISBN: 0-913678-13-9

Copyright © 1976 by The New Day Press, Karamu House
2355 East 89th Street, Cleveland, Ohio
44106

2nd Printing, 1980

MEET THE CONTRIBUTORS

CECELIA HOWARD
BALDRIDGE is a two-time
contributor to *New Day*. She
is a free-lance commercial
artist.

EBRASKA CEASOR is a
kindergarten teacher at
Chambers Elementary School
in East Cleveland. In 1974,
she was named Ohio Teacher
of the Year.

FANNIE DILLARD was born in Birmingham, Alabama but came to Cleveland before she was a year old. The story in this book is her first published work. She is presently a beautician.

CHARLOTTE DURANT is a teacher at Charles Waddell Chesnutt Elementary School and thus has a special interest in the story she illustrated.

ARDELIA DIXON recently retired from the Cleveland Public School System. She received a B.A. degree in English from Cleveland College of Case Western Reserve University in Cleveland, Ohio.

HELEN LYNUM EVANS is a psychologist for the Warrensville Center for the Mentally Retarded. She is a graduate of Wellesley College in Massachusetts and received her M.A. from Ohio State in 1972.

BRENDA JOHNSTON has appeared in all of the *New Day Press* publications. She is also the author of a novel for children and a book for *Scholastic*. She is presently completing requirements for the B.A. in Education at Case Western Reserve University.

MARY SHEPARD's stories have also appeared in *New Day*'s earlier publications. She has also published a book of religious poetry. Aside from her writing, she is active in church and civic circles.

RON SMITH has been a prolific contributor to New Day since its inception. He is a caseworker for the Cuyahoga County Welfare Department and a free-lance commercial artist.

DAVID WILSON is a free-lance writer and poet as well as a painter. Film-making is another of his interests.

TABLE OF CONTENTS

Lucy Bagby Johnson: A Fugitive Slave's Flight to Freedom

by Helen Lynum Evans

Illustrated by Ron Smith

LUCY BAGBY JOHNSON:
A FUGITIVE SLAVE'S FLIGHT TO FREEDOM

by

Helen Lynum Evans

"Lucy, chile, Miss Goshorn wants you in her bedroom."

"What she wont now? I jus' fixed her bath water."

"Gal, you better git in there 'fore she get mad. You know how she is."

"Yes, ma'am." Lucy left the Goshorns' large kitchen table where she was helping her mother to peel potatoes. She went through the corridor past the dining room and up the winding stairs to Melissa Goshorn's room. She could smell the fragrance of Melissa's gardenia perfume as she knocked on the door.

"Lucy, that you? Come on in." Lucy walked into Melissa's bedroom. There stood Melissa struggling to fasten her corset.

"Help me fasten this thing." Lucy fastened the last four hooks on her corset. She began to have a longing to live like Melissa. At seventeen, their lives were so different. Melissa was free to go to balls and dance all night while Lucy worked. She wished she could leave Virginia. Maybe buy her freedom. Anything to get away from the constant feelings of being a prisoner.

"Lucy, are you listening to me?"

"M'am? Oh, Miss Melissa, I'm sorry. I wuz thinkin' how pretty you look."

"Lucinda Bagby, you couldn't be listenin'. I'm goin' to Pittsburgh next month, Papa wants me to take a girl along. I want you to go."

"Oh, Miss Melissa, I can't wait to go!"

"Yes, it's goin' to be a lot of fun. I'm going to attend several dances with my cousins. And we'll see lots of fancy places."

So in June, 1852, Lucy and her master's daughter boarded a train to Pittsburgh. The two young girls traveled in a special car which belonged to the Goshorns. There was a small section partitioned off for Lucy to sleep.

For Lucy the most exciting part of the train ride was breakfast time. All the blacks had to eat together in the back of the train. She had a chance to meet some free blacks. Her strong black hands were sweating when she opened the door to the "colored" eating area. She was so happy to hear the voices of the blacks in the crowded little room. She found a seat sandwiched between a very large woman and a rather slender man. While Lucy ate, the man answered her questions about how he had gained his freedom.

He had come North on the Underground Railroad. Lucy listened but she knew this would not work for her. His escape was before the passage of the Fugitive Slave Law. This law required northern states to return slaves to their owners. Still Lucy dreamed of escaping some day in the future.

At the train depot, Mr. John Goshorn, one of Melissa's cousins, and his carriage driver met them. A tall, husky man, Mr. Goshorn hugged Melissa so forcefully she was lifted off her feet.

The carriage driver stood quietly behind Mr. Goshorn. Lucy saw him wink once at her. Yet he never lost his solemn composure. She smiled at him. The carriage had a separate seat for Melissa and Mr. Goshorn. Lucy sat in the front with the driver.

At the Goshorns' home, Lucy went with Tylus, the carriage driver, to the servants' quarters. Their living area was on the second floor of the carriage house. Tylus introduced Lucy to Anne, the other Goshorn servant. She was to sleep in the same room with Anne.

That first night Anne and Lucy stayed up late talking. Lucy was fascinated with the idea of receiving money for work. She wanted to be free to go and come as she pleased. Anne tried to tell her some of the problems of the blacks in the North, but to her nothing Anne said was as bad as slavery.

Although Lucy was busy helping Melissa to get ready for parties and dinners, she did have a chance to go to church with

Tylus and Anne. The church was in the black section of Pittsburgh. Lucy was impressed with the redstone church. Tylus told her the church members had built it.

After the church services all the people stood around the churchyard talking. Tylus took Lucy over to meet a group of his friends. Lucy had her eyes on the tallest man in the group, when Tylus said, "Lucy, I want you to meet George Johnson and James McNeil. They're two people who can help you if you ever want to come North."

"Yeah, we love helping pretty misses like you, ma'am. Where you come from?" asked George, the tall one.

Looking down, she said, "Wheeling, Virginia." She felt warm and shy all of a sudden. Being nearly six feet, she seldom met men who were taller than she. George looked very handsome to her.

"Wheeling? I know several men there. They're part of the Underground Railroad. They can help you to start on your way North. When you go to their homes, they can take you to the next home on the Underground Railroad."

"No, George. I'm scared to leave. The last man left wuz brought home. My master beat him nearly to death." By this time the others had drifted away. Lucy and George were standing alone.

"Is it any better to stay? Don't they beat people who stay? Won't they sell your babies if you have any?"

"Ya, I know it's bad. But so far I've been lucky. Me, my mother and my sister are together. They sold Papa when I wuz a baby."

"Don't you know your luck may change? We ain't nothing to them. They'll sell you, too."

"When that day comes that they sell one of us, I'm leavin'. I'll risk death before they sell me."

On the way home from church Lucy kept thinking of George and his plans. She knew life was better in the North. Yet was it worth risking death?

Lucy went back to Wheeling with Melissa. Often while

working for the Goshorns, she thought of escaping. In 1857 things began to happen, which gave her the courage to leave. That year Mr. Goshorn decided to send Lucy to live in town with his forty-three-year-old son.

The younger Goshorn had often said Lucy was a pretty wench. Most of the time Mr. Goshorn's wife and three teen-age children were keeping Lucy busy. One day when she was alone with Mr. Goshorn, he tried to kiss her.

The next weekend Lucy was at old Mr. Goshorn's house to help serve for a party. She told her mother about her unhappy life at the younger Goshorn's home. Her mother pleaded with old Mr. Goshorn to let Lucy come back to the plantation. He refused. Her mother became angry. She cursed him. After this, Mr. Goshorn sold Lucy's mother and sister to his cousin in North Carolina. With her people gone, Lucy had no reason to stay.

At night Lucy slept fitfully. She woke up exhausted. The cries and pleas of her mother and sister were ever-present memories. And her life was still sad in the younger Goshorn's home.

Lucy walked away from the Goshorns' house in October, 1860. She had nothing but the clothes on her back. She walked until near daylight. Hungry and tired, she stopped and went into the woods to rest. She could not relax. Her mind kept telling her to move on. She knew the Goshorns would miss her in a few hours. Old Mr. Goshorn was sure to send some men to find her.

Her fears caused her to start walking again. Finally, she took a chance and stopped at the home of an old slave on a nearby farm. Here she learned of a man in the next town who would help her.

When Lucy reached this home, the man's wife welcomed her. They gave her some food. Then they hid her in a secret room behind their fireplace. All night she lay trembling. Every time she heard noises, her stomach tightened. It would be a long journey, but Lucy was willing to try to make it.

The next morning the owner of the farm put Lucy in a compartment of his wagon, covered it with hay, and took her to another home. She went from place to place along the Underground Railroad until she reached Marietta, Ohio. From Marietta, a black man and his wife took her to Cleveland. They introduced Lucy to Mr. L. A. Benton. The Bentons paid Lucy to cook and clean for them.

Wherever Lucy went in Cleveland, she saw signs announcing rewards for slaves. One day while walking to a store, Lucy was warned of signs in Pennsylvania which offered $220 for information about her. She found it hard to believe the man who told her. She thought some of her friends would have heard of the search for her.

On the afternoon of January 19, 1861, there was a loud noise at the Bentons' front door. Lucy was serving dinner. Suddenly a U.S. deputy and Mr. Goshorn broke the door to the Bentons' home. Lucy screamed when they rushed into the Bentons' dining room.

Mr. Benton rose and asked, "What's goin' on here? Have you lost your mind? What reason do you have for breaking into my house?"

"We have a warrant for the arrest of this fugitive slave! Come on, gal!"

They pulled Lucy outside and threw her into their carriage. She cried and pleaded for her freedom on the way to the jailhouse. They took her by both arms to pull her out of the carriage. She was placed in a small cell with a cot and wash pan.

The next day Mr. L. A. Benton came to see Lucy. He brought Judge Spalding, one of Cleveland's most prominent lawyers, with him. The judge volunteered to help Lucy. Three days later, a hearing was to be held in the government building on Rockwell Street. When the five deputies took Lucy from the jailhouse, a crowd of blacks and whites were outside. They yelled names at the deputies.

As their chant to free Lucy grew louder, Emiline Sous, a friend of Lucy's, stepped forward, and threw pepper into one of the deputy's eyes. Another deputy arrested Emeline. She was later fined one cent by a judge who did not believe in slavery. The guards reached the courthouse and Judge Tilden heard the case. Although he felt sorry for Lucy, the laws of the nation compelled him to send the case to trial in the Federal Court.

On the day of the trial, one hundred and fifty deputies took Lucy to the Federal Courthouse. There was no chance for anyone to help her to escape. Commissioner White ruled in favor of her owner. He had a bill of sale to prove his ownership. While she stood speechless after the verdict, the commissioner offered to give one hundred dollars toward Lucy's freedom. Mr. Goshorn refused to accept the money.

Back in Wheeling, Mr. Goshorn had Lucy beaten and placed in jail. Later he sent her to Charleston, Virginia. She worked for his cousin, who was kind to her. Prior to the outbreak of the Civil War, Mr. Goshorn's cousin sent Lucy farther South with one of his white workers. In Fayetteville, Tennessee, they stopped to purchase tickets to continue their journey. A group of Union Army soldiers came to the train depot while they were there. The white Southerners at the depot were looking very frightened.

Lucy saw one of the soldiers coming toward her. He said, "Where you going, young lady?"

Looking toward the floor, she said, "I'm with my master's overseer, sir." Her heart beat fast as she wondered if the soldier might free her.

"I'm Captain Vance from the Union Army. Didn't you all hear about the Emancipation Proclamation?"

"This woman is a slave, Yankee." The overseer was standing with an angry look on his face. There was no way he could fight all twenty of the troopers.

"Mister, watch your mouth. This woman is free to go wherever she wants to go. President Lincoln has proclaimed the end of slavery."

"You mean I'm free, Mister?"

"Yes, ma'am." The Captain gave Lucy some money to buy a train ticket. She went to Athens, Ohio, where she worked until

8

she had enough money to go to Pittsburgh.

While working in a dry goods store, Lucy met George Johnson again. He was dressed in a Union Army uniform. Until the Civil War ended, he stayed in touch with her. At the end of the war, they married. Then, looking for better work, George Johnson and his wife moved to Cleveland.

In Cleveland, Lucy was often treated like a celebrity. People respected and honored her for struggling so hard to gain her freedom. She is remembered in Ohio's history because of her fight for liberation.

Bibliography

Annals of the Early Settlers Association of Cleveland, Vol. 5. Cleveland: Published by Early Settlers' Association of Cleveland, Ohio, 1904.

Buckmaster, Henrietta, *Let My People Go: The Story of the Underground Railroad and the Growth of the Abolition Movement.* Boston: Beacon Press, 1959.

The Cleveland Leader, January 24, 1861; February 13 and 14, 1861.

Child, L. Maria, edit., *Incidents in the Life of a Slave Girl.* New York: Harcourt, Brace, 1973.

Davis, Russell H., *Black Americans in Ohio's City of Cleveland.* Cleveland: Western Reserve Historical Society, 1972.

Davis, Russell H., *Memorable Negroes in Cleveland's Past.* Cleveland: Western Reserve Historical Society, 1969, p. 23-29.

Charles Waddell Chesnutt

by Fannie Dillard

Illustrated by Charlotte Durant

CHARLES WADDELL CHESNUTT

by

Fannie L. Dillard

In 1856 a wagon train made its slow and arduous journey from Fayetteville, North Carolina toward Ohio. This was not the usual wagon train, for the travelers were free Black people. Danger and bitter hardship dogged their trail. The fear of Indians and hostile white marauders cast a blight over their spirits, but the hope for a better life, a life free of oppression, spurred them on.

Among the passengers was a young lady named Ann Maria Sampson, who was traveling with her mother, Chloe Sampson. Maria was a gay, energetic, and determined young woman who absolutely refused to entertain the idea of turning back. She did all she could to cheer and encourage everyone around her. One of her fellow travelers, Andrew Jackson Chesnutt, found her wit and charm irresistible. The two young people fell deeply in love. However, Jack went to Indiana to an uncle and Maria and her mother to Cleveland, Ohio.

Chloe Sampson bought a little cottage on Hudson Street in a German neighborhood. Maria felt happy and secure in her new life, but she could not forget Jack. In Indiana, Jack's uncle was trying to help him with his education. Jack found it impossible to get his mind off Maria, and the next year he left Indiana and went to Cleveland. On July 26, 1857, Ann Maria Sampson and Andrew Jackson Chesnutt were married. The young couple settled down with Maria's mother in the little house on Hudson Street. Jack found a job as a driver-conductor on a horsecar. Maria and Jack were happy and contented. Their first child, Charles Waddell, was born on June 20, 1858. Maria's heart and mind were filled with love and grand dreams for her first-born. The two were to share a close and loving relationship throughout her lifetime.

With the baby's future in mind, Jack and Maria moved to

15

Oberlin to be near Oberlin College. Another son, Lewis, was born in Oberlin. However, Jack soon realized that Cleveland was a better place to earn a living, so they returned there. Jack got his old job back and Maria welcomed her mother's help with the two babies. In time another son, Andrew, was born. Later, a baby girl, who died in infancy.

When the Civil War broke out, Jack joined the Union Army as a teamster. At the end of the war his father promised to open a grocery store for him in Fayetteville if he would come back to North Carolina. Over the protests of his upset wife, he accepted. Maria Chesnutt wanted her sons to obtain a good education. Only her first-born, Charles, shared his mother's respect for knowledge. The rest of the family considered this somewhat of a joke. Young Charles attended Howard School, which had been built and maintained mostly by Blacks, including his father. He had to help in the store and keep up his chores at home.

Maria gave birth to three more girls — Clara, Mary, and Lillian. After the birth of Lillian, Maria's health failed steadily. When not in school or working at the store, Charles washed clothes, cleaned house, took care of the younger children and any other chore that would take some of the burden from his ailing mother. When he was thirteen years old, his mother became bedfast and finally died. Maria's mother, who had come to nurse her daughter and care for her grandchildren during her daughter's illness, asked Jack to let a young niece, Mary Ochiltree, come and take care of the children. In return she was to attend Howard School. This arrangement was short-lived, however. Jack and Mary decided to marry. Cousin Mary was very kind to the children and took good care of them.

Soon the family was again increasing. At this time the store began to show financial reverses and Jack finally lost it. He moved his family to a farm and told Charles he would have to give up school to help support the family. One of his father's friends offered Charles a job in his saloon keeping the books and doing odd jobs. This was the end of his mother's dreams and hopes for him. Charles's spirit was crushed and he was heartbroken. Sadly he told Robert Harris, the principal of Howard School, that he was leaving to work in a saloon to add to the family income. Mr. Harris had taken his prize pupil under his wing after the death of Charles's mother. He was so shaken by this news he dismissed the class and went to Charles's father's farm to talk with him. Harris reached an agreement with Charles's father for Charles to work as an assistant teacher at the school. His small salary would be turned over to his father.

Charles worked first at Howard and later at other area Black schools that could use him. On weekends he worked as a country peddler. He realized now that he could not finish high school. Away from home most of the time and lonely, Charles began to study on his own. He studied algebra, natural philosophy, theory of education, Latin, American history, and literature. He read classics and the Bible.

In 1877, Robert Harris was named principal of the new State Normal School for Black teachers located on the second floor of Howard School. Chesnutt became first assistant to Robert Harris.

Romance now entered Chesnutt's life. Teaching at Howard School was Miss Susan V. Perry, the daughter of a well-to-do barbershop proprietor. Charles began to spend most of his spare time at the Perry house. On June 6, 1878, Susan V. Perry and Charles W. Chesnutt were married. They set up housekeeping in two rooms of the large Perry house. The following year their first child, Ethel, was born.

Inspired by his little family, Chesnutt applied himself with new zeal to his program of self-education. To his knowledge of organ and piano, he added German, French and shorthand. He still found time to make a garden and spend time with his wife and baby. Chesnutt was a man who always cherished and loved his family.

Robert Harris died in 1881 and Chesnutt became principal of Howard School at the salary of seventy-five dollars per month. He now earned more money than any other Black in Fayetteville.

17

Charles and Susan Chesnutt were able to move into a home of their own. Another girl, Helen Maria, was born. A woman was hired to help Susan with the housework.

Chesnutt's brilliant mind, that in years to come would make him an inspiration to his race, set him apart at that time. He was a quiet, retiring man and his superior education made it difficult to find someone with whom he could converse and discuss various books, subjects, and philosophies. To a great extent his life was a lonely and frustrating one. Because he was a very light-skinned Black man, educated whites oftimes mistook him for a Caucasian, and would talk with him. However, when they were told he was a Black man, they usually became indignant. He grew tired of having to accept the put-downs and slurs of the North Carolina whites and decided to move North for his social benefit and the social and educational benefit of his children and his wife, who by now was expecting their third child.

Chesnutt had always wanted to become a writer and he determined to work toward this end. He felt that the printed page could bring better understanding and a more equal and amiable relationship between the races. He resigned his position and left Fayetteville and went to New York City where he became reporter for Dow Jones and Company. He spent five lonely months there working and writing.

In 1884 he moved on to Cleveland and in April of that year his family joined him. While working for the Nickel Plate Railroad as a clerk, and later as a stenographer to Judge Samuel Williamson, the firm's legal counsel, he studied law and in 1887 passed the Ohio Bar with the highest grade in his group. However, he never actually practiced law. Three years later he established a legal stenographic service which became very prosperous. This provided him with a secure income for his family. Now he could give more time to writing.

Although he had received many rejections, he continued to submit his stories and articles to various magazine and newspaper editors. In 1885 his first story, "Uncle Peter's House", was printed

Charlotte T. Durant

in the Cleveland *News and Herald*. In 1887 "The Goophered Grapevine" appeared in the *Atlantic Monthly*. This was literary history. He was the first Afro-American to become a professional writer. Chesnutt made no attempt to hide his race, but only in close literary circles was his race known. In September 1891, he informed the Houghton Mifflin Publishing Company that he was Afro-American. The publishers withheld this information from the public until 1899 because they respected his right to personal privacy and because they were concerned about the public's reception to his early works.

The publication of *The Conjure Women, Wife of His Youth,* and *Frederick Douglass*, all in 1899, launched his writing and lecturing career. These early works were well received by leading critics of the day, as well as by the general public. Anticipating well-deserved financial rewards from his writings, Chesnutt closed his stenographic service. He was now forty-one years old. His two older daughters, Ethel and Helen, were in college. His son, Edwin, was in high school. The late addition and baby of the family, Dorothy, was just starting school

As Chesnutt continued to write, it was apparent that most of his stories centered in and around Fayetteville, North Carolina. Groveland, another locale used in stories, is obviously Cleveland. In most of his stories he tried to put across a message about the relationship of the oppressed Blacks and their white oppressors in a humorous but satirical way. Yet, in 1901, he reopened his legal stenography firm because he did not receive the recognition his writing skill deserved. There were many reasons for this, including the fact that many white readers rejected his frank treatment of "passing" and race-mixing themes in such stories as *The House Behind the Cedars*, published in 1900. There is also the fact that at that time too few Black people could afford to buy enough books to support him. He was not a radical man, but in his quiet way he was a champion of his people. He wrote letters of protest to government officials whom he hoped would see the need for racial fair play and speak up when necessary.

Chesnutt's last book, *The Colonel's Dream*, was published in 1905. He continued to write essays and articles for various newspapers and magazines. By the time of his death on November 15, 1932, he was credited with fifty-three essays and speeches, six novels, eighteen short stories, five poems and one play.

In 1904 Charles and Susan Chesnutt purchased the type of home they had always dreamed of owning. The house stood at 1668 Lamont Street. With his wife Susan at his side Chesnutt began to enter the social, literary and musical circles. Charles Chesnutt was elected to the all-white Tresart Club, a group of musicians, writers and painters, and the exclusive all-male Rowfant Club which is now located at 3028 Prospect. He spent many happy Saturday evenings with learned book lovers in this club. The Chesnutts were also members of The Social Circle, a very exclusive club of highly educated Blacks. Of course, Chesnutt joined these social organizations because he found in them individuals who shared his love of literature and music. Yet he chided them for their snobbery: for example, the Rowfant Club members in "Baxter's Procrustes."

Chesnutt was involved in many other local groups including the Cleveland Chamber of Commerce, the Cleveland Bar Association, the Cleveland Council on Sociology, the Playhouse Settlement, now famous Karamu House (also serving as its presiding officer.)

In 1905 he was the only Clevelander to receive an invitation to Mark Twain's seventieth birthday party given by Colonel George Harvey at Delmonico's restaurant in New York City. This was one of the most outstanding events in the history of American literary society. He was elected to the National Arts Club in 1917. He received an honorary L.L.D. degree from Wilberforce University when he spoke there in 1913. The N.A.A.C.P. awarded him the Springarn Medal in 1928 for "Pioneer work as a literary artist depicting the life and struggles of Americans of Negro descent, and for his long and useful career as a scholar, worker, and free man of one of America's greatest cities."

21

Bibliography

Adams, Russell L., *Great Negroes Past and Present.* Chicago: Afro-Am Press, 1969.

Chesnutt, Helen M., Charles Waddell Chesnutt: *Pioneer of the Color Line.* Chapel Hill: University of North Carolina Press, 1952.

Render, Sylvia Lyons, *The Short Fiction of Charles W. Chesnutt.* Washington, D.C.: Howard University Press, 1974.

Jane Edna Hunter

by Brenda A. Johnson

Illustrated by Ron Smith

JANE EDNA HUNTER
Founder of the Phillis Wheatley Association

by
Brenda A. Johnston

"Jane, honey, don't look at me like that."

"Like what?" snapped Jane.

"Like you can't stand me, honey." At Jane's annoyed look, her mother stammered. "You know what I mean," she said.

"I don't," answered Jane and turned away. She had been thinking as she looked at her mother how glad she was that she did not look like her. Jane Hunter's mother was dark-skinned and to Jane that meant the same as ugly. Jane had taken her own coloring more after her father than her mother. Her father had looked like a white man. Still he had been a slave until freed by the Emancipation Proclamation. Jane's mother had been born the day the document had been signed.

Jane's family eked out a poor and drab existence as tenant farmers near Pendleton, South Carolina. But in spite of this, Jane's father had always encouraged her to go to school. When he died, however, Jane had managed to finish only the fourth grade even though she was fourteen.

Things had always been hard even while Jane's father lived, but now they were much worse. Jane did domestic work in the homes of white people. Even though she worked as best she could, she could not please them. Already she had been fired several times.

"You sure you want to leave, honey?" Jane's mother asked her.

"Yes!" snapped Jane. After a moment she said bitterly, "I can't stand being a sharecropper like you all my life. People who work share ain't no better than dirt."

"Sure, it's hard work. But so is the work you're doing for

25

the white folk. They ain't going to do nothing but work you to death."

"If you ain't a sharecropper, hard work will get you somewhere," Jane answered. "That's what Daddy always said. But if you're a sharecropper, hard work will kill you. Just like it killed him."

Jane's mother looked hurt. Jane felt bad when she saw the pain in her mother's face. She couldn't help it. She really loved her mother deeply.

"Well, I'm on my way," said Jane, picking up the paper bag that contained her belongings. Her mother looked sadder and more tired than ever. Jane was relieved to leave, but she thought to herself, "Poor, poor black woman." She could never wipe away the memory of her mother sadly watching her leave.

Jane went to live and work for Rev. and Mrs. Williams at a nearby missionary school. She managed to finish junior high school when she was 17. She continued to do domestic work for years in the homes of white people. Although the work was hard and the hours long, Jane was a perfectionist. She always did more work than was required and worked harder and longer than was expected.

One day her employer, Mrs. Ellen Hunt, a prominent woman in the community, said to her, "Jane, why don't you make something of yourself?"

"Like what?" Jane answered, not looking up from her dusting.

"Something worthwhile. You most certainly are not cut out to be just a cleaning woman or servant."

"I don't mind," laughed Jane.

Mrs. Hunt looked at her queerly. "I think I believe you," she said. "Yes, I do. And it's hard to believe. You're a rare person, Jane."

Jane smiled pleasantly.

"Still, Jane, a person like yourself should have a career." Mrs. Hunt was silent for a few moments, then her face lit up.

"Jane, have you ever thought of becoming a nurse?"

"A nurse?" Jane asked.

"Yes. It would be perfect. You know how to meet the needs of people and you love doing it."

"I haven't finished enough school to be a nurse," Jane said.

"But you're young. Finish school. It's perfect," Mrs. Hunt insisted.

"I'll think about it," Jane answered. And she did think. When she made up her mind that Mrs. Hunt was right, Jane moved to Charleston, South Carolina. She worked until she could enter Hampton Institute in Virginia. When she graduated, she was a trained nurse.

But becoming a nurse did not satisfy Jane long. Her memories of extreme poverty could not be forgotten. She felt her hope for a better future would be forever lost as long as she stayed in the South. Reminders that black people were nobody were everywhere. Bathrooms, movies, restaurants, and busses were filled with signs saying "white only" or "colored".

One day as Jane rode home in the "colored" section of the bus, she thought to herself, "I would love to live somewhere where I would never have to see another "white" or "colored" sign. She had heard that in the North things were better. The more Jane thought about it, the more she liked the idea of moving from the South. She chose Cleveland, Ohio, as her new home.

When Jane did move to Cleveland in 1905, she was relieved that no "colored" or "white" signs were posted. She learned, however, that Cleveland had unwritten laws that separated the black and white people from each other. Since Jane did not wish to live in the "lower class" black neighborhoods, she looked for living quarters in "nice" neighborhoods. Her applications were always turned down. In the end, she had to live in the "black belt," the east side of Cleveland. The crime rate was high, the living conditions were poor, and there were an overwhelming number of juvenile delinquents.

Jane then spent day after lonely day hunting for a job as a

27

nurse. She didn't understand why no one would hire her until one doctor told her frankly that no doctor would hire a "nigger" nurse. At first Jane was outraged at the doctor's rudeness. Later, she was thankful. When she went job hunting the next day, she told the woman she would take any job open.

The woman brightened. "We do have a job open for someone who can give massages."

Jane smiled back. "I would love that," she said. To herself she thought how different it was in the North. In the South, black nurses had no trouble at all getting jobs. In fact, black nurses were hired faster than white ones.

Jane took the job and, as usual, she worked hard. One of the girls she met while working was a secretary to John D. Rockefeller, Cleveland's famous millionaire. When the girl learned that Jane was a trained nurse, she recommended her to a prominent surgeon. The surgeon hired Jane. Afterwards, she had no trouble at all getting better-paying jobs. With better jobs, she was able to move into the middle-class black neighborhoods where only professional blacks lived. Jane was glad to move away from the neighborhood filled with lonely young women who came from the South to find jobs. She was relieved to forget about the youngsters who roamed the streets because they had nowhere else to go. She knew that life would be filled with trouble for these people, but she had managed to escape.

But escape from the black belt did not give Jane the contentment and joy she had expected. Now that her long struggle to be somebody was over, Jane wondered if it had been worth the price she had paid. All her life she had been obsessed with pleasing white people. She had always been trying to prove that she was different from other blacks, even her own mother. The thought of how she had lived her life began to torment Jane.

"I'm going to be different," Jane vowed to herself. "I'm going to start all over again. When did this running away from myself all begin?" With a sudden fit of guilt, Jane remembered where it all began. It had started years ago when she bade goodbye to a very weary, dark-skinned woman who looked as if her heart were breaking. Her mother! "Oh, Mother," Jane thought to herself. "Forgive me. I'm so sorry. I'll make it up to you. I'll show you." Jane made plans to return home at once.

But all of Jane's plans of redeeming herself were cruelly and suddenly interrupted. Death took her mother before Jane could tell her how very much she loved and respected her. Guilt tormented Jane and she suffered heartbreaking grief. Jane did not know how she managed to keep working, but she did.

It was while at work one day that the cleaning woman asked Jane to help her niece find a place to stay while she looked for a job. Jane thought of her mother when she looked at the woman.

"Has she tried the Y.W.C.A.?" she asked, kindly.

"They ain't going to let no blacks in there," the woman replied. Jane's mind went back to her early days in Cleveland and her hard time trying to find a room.

"Too bad there's not a 'Y' for black girls," she said aloud. As soon as she had spoken, Jane was inspired. Long after the cleaning woman had gone, Jane was lost in thought. "If some of the opportunities that white people have were open to us, we wouldn't have to depend on their good will to be successful."

Jane was willing to do anything to save other black girls from losing their pride and self-respect as she had. It was time for blacks like herself and her successful friends to help those who couldn't help themselves.

Jane shared her idea of starting a rooming house for black girls with her friends. "Oh, no," one of them told her promptly. "That's just segregating blacks more than ever. What we should be working to do is to integrate them into white society."

"We can't keep waiting for that," Jane answered. "Or at least," she added quickly, "while we're waiting, we can do something for ourselves."

Jane's friends would not help her so she went on with her dream alone. She was to say years later that all she had was "a nickel and a prayer." But in the year 1911 Jane opened a rooming

29

house on 40th and Central Avenue in Cleveland. She called it the Working Girls Association. It was soon packed to overflowing.

Jane's idea was to give young black women a decent place to live. But she soon learned that most of the girls who came to her needed to be trained in some skill if they were to find any kind of job. She began a program of teaching the girls domestic skills. Jane, like Booker T. Washington, had been educated at Hampton. Both had learned there that domestic education for blacks would receive financial support from the white community. Booker T. Washington had used this knowledge to gain white support when he founded Tuskegee Institute, a black college in Alabama. So now Jane turned to the white community for support in educating black girls for domestic work. It was a wise decision, and John D. Rockefeller himself donated $100,000 to the program.

When the education program became part of the rooming house, it served more than just working girls. So the name was changed to the Phillis Wheatley Association in honor of the ex-slave who had become a famous poet. As the school continued to grow and receive support, Jane was able to offer the girls an education that included art and literature as well as domestic skills. She later started a Girls' Reserve for black girls between the ages of 12 and 18. For the first time, many girls who had never had the opportunity to be in the Girl Scouts and hike and camp were given that chance.

The Phillis Wheatley Association finally offered the black community of Cleveland a cafeteria, an employment office, a nursery school, a health education program, a music school, and a monthly newsletter, "The Open Door." The Association even became a training ground for Case Western Reserve University students working on masters' degrees at the School of Applied Social Sciences.

Not only did the school progress over the years, but so did Jane. In 1925 she became a lawyer. She was already a nurse. And her work with the Phillis Wheatley Association made her a leading social worker. Near the end of her life, when Jane was ready to retire, she raised $75,000 and set up a scholarship fund for black high school students.

When her life was over, Jane's tribute to the memory of her mother lived on as concrete monument of black pride and accomplishment. And now social service agencies like the Phillis Wheatley Association can be found in almost every major city in the United States.

Bibliography

Davis, Russell, "Memorable Negroes," *Cleveland Plain Dealer,* August 3, 1969.

Hunter, Jane, *A Nickel and a Prayer*, Cleveland: Elli Kane Publishing Co., 1940.

Granville T. Woods
The Successful Dropout

by Mary L. Shepard

Illustrated by Cecelia Howard Baldridge

GRANVILLE T. WOODS,
THE SUCCESSFUL DROPOUT

by

Mary L. Shepard

Mrs. Woods set the hot iron upright on the end of the ironing board while she rearranged the pair of bluejeans she was ironing. Surrounded by text books, Granville sat on the well-worn sofa. He was ten years old and her second oldest son. His mind was not on the homework he was supposed to be doing. He was staring beyond the books at the iron as his mother set it down and, using pads, picked it up again to resume her ironing.

Granville's mother talked while she ironed. "You're too young to even be thinking about quitting school. You just got started and haven't learned half of what you should know yet." Her words barely penetrated Granville's thoughts, although he had heard them spoken so many times by his best friends, as well as by relatives.

While Granville valued the opinions of those genuinely concerned about him, he was also determined to achieve the goals he had set for himself. He was very sure of what he wanted his future career to be and willing to work very hard to achieve those career goals. Yet the trouble was that no one believed in him. Everyone thought that if he left school to find apprentice work, his education would end. Granville had to prove it the hard way, but was not too concerned about convincing anyone except his parents. He needed their approval to quit school.

"I asked what you are going to use for money to get all this training?" He heard his mother raise her voice and he realized that he must somehow make his mother understand the way he felt. He searched for words to convey his feelings to her, but the words didn't come. He merely said, "Ma, I just can't make it work for me at school. I'm failing in English and I can't seem to get

35

interested in anything but electricity and things I can operate with my hands."

"That's exactly what I mean," Granville's mother answered. "You're failing in school already. How can you expect to make it in anything else without school learning?"

Granville stretched out on the sofa and picked up a magazine on electronics. He slowly thumbed through the pages, feeling the excitement begin to flow through him as it always did when he read about all the wonderful new things happening in the world of electricity. He peeped out from behind the pages of the magazine at his mother. She seemed intent on her ironing but her expression told Granville that she was not satisfied with his answer. He felt even more motivated by the fact that he held proof in his hands of the importance of new ideas in the field he was interested in. An article he had just read was about the collision of two trains which had been caused by the lack of communication between the train engineers.

Granville began talking to his mother as if the conversation had not lapsed. "Ma, just picking up this book and reading about all the electrical inventions and the need for more and better ideas makes me much more determined to work toward the goal of putting my ideas to work for me. I watched you iron and wondered if there wasn't a way to make that iron function better, like evenly controlling the heat so you wouldn't have to keep going back to heat it on the stove."

Granville had found the words he needed to convince his mother. He sat upright and talked steadily now. He had a new look in his eyes that his mother could not interpret. She was so surprised at his outburst that she stopped the iron right where it was—on the seat of the bluejeans. When she finally smelled the scorched denim, she snatched the iron off the pants. Then she managed to smile.

"Well, I guess I'd better have another talk with your father when he gets home from work, because you sure have convinced me — and cost me a patch on the seat of these jeans."

With his mother, Granville finally succeeded in also convincing his father of the sincerity of his desire. Both parents wanted the best for their son and she had given the matter of his leaving school much thought. While they admired his courage, they were a bit skeptical as to how successful he might be. They lacked the financial means to back him up, but eventually felt that he deserved the chance to prove himself. After all, he did show so much promise in the mechanics of electricity. They gave their permission for their young son to drop out of school. Granville was very happy and grateful at the show of their hard-won faith.

He scouted around the city, inquiring at every electrical mechanical shop trying to find just the right place to begin his training. When he had narrowed his choices down to two, he approached the owners with his proposition. The first one laughed him right out of the shop.

"I wouldn't hire anybody as young as you. And how do you expect to make any impression on a potential employer by dropping out of school? That's a foolish thing to do." Granville was not able to change his mind.

Granville was more fortunate at the second place he visited. The owner recognized the qualities of a genius in Granville and admired his determination to get ahead and his willingness to work hard at it. He hired Granville on the spot.

As a machine and blacksmith apprentice, Granville worked hard and learned well. Wanting to learn a lot more at a much faster rate, he then decided that he did need schooling but of a different kind. He started attending night school while he served his apprenticeship. This was very hard for him, but even though he was so often exhausted, his determination pushed him on.

When his family moved from his native Ohio in 1872, Granville was progressing with great strides and felt he needed more practical experience in order to gain more extensive knowledge. He got a job as a fireman on the Iron Mountain Railroad in Missouri. He was then sixteen years old. Always feeling he needed to learn more and more, he continued searching for new ways to broaden his knowledge. In his spare time he studied electricity and from his small earnings he paid a master mechanic to tutor him.

In 1874 Granville decided he was ready for college so he got a job in a rolling mill where he earned much more than ever before. He saved all the money he could. Then he moved to Springfield, Illinois where he enrolled as a special student and took courses in electrical and mechanical engineering for two years.

At the age of twenty-two he went to sea early in 1878 as an engineer on the British steamer, Ironsides. At sea for several years, he visited many parts of the world studying electrical inventions and comparing them with others he had seen. He became fascinated with thermal power and electricity as a source of energy. The use of these powers triggered his imagination and made him eager to put his ideas into practical use.

Returning to America in 1880, he ran a locomotive on the Danville and Southern Railroad for a while. Woods then settled in Cincinnati, Ohio and took out his first patent in 1884, for a steam boiler furnace. Next he invented an apparatus called a "Telephone Transmission," which made it possible to transmit messages by electricity. The American Bell Telephone Company eventually bought this patent from Woods.

Granville T. Woods had finally made it. After years of working hard to prepare himself, he was ready to really express himself through his electrical genius. In Cincinnati he formed his own company, the Woods Electrical Company. There he manufactured and sold telephone, telegraph and electrical instruments.

His most important invention was "The Induction Telegraph System," in 1887. This gadget made it possible for many trains to communicate with station operators. This Synchronous Multiplex Railway Telegraph System made railroad travel much safer by permitting dispatchers to note at a glance the position of any rolling trains. Collisions could be more easily averted.

The Edison and Phelps Company challenged Woods in court two separate times, each time claiming priority for Thomas Edison, who was working on a similar device. Woods won both times, being certified by the United States Patent Office as the inventor. Edison then offered Woods a job on his staff, but the proud, hard-working, self-made man was not about to take second place in the field in which he had struggled so hard to excel. He turned Edison down.

Woods' inventions included a polarized relay, automatic safety cut-out for electric circuits, amusement apparatus, electric incubator and the automatic air brake for trains. A regulator for electric motors and other important inventions made a total of more than fifty patents that Granville T. Woods took out in his lifetime, exceeding the output of any other black inventor of his time.

Eventually Woods closed his factory in Cincinnati and moved to New York City, where he concentrated on inventing until he died there on January 30, 1910, at the age of fifty-four.

Most of his patents were sold to major American firms such as General Electric Company, Westinghouse, and the Bell Telephone Company.

Bibliography

Plaski and Brown (Ed.), *The Negro Almanac*, New York: Bellwether, 1967.

Toppin, Edgar A., *A Biographical History of Blacks in America Since 1528*, New York: David McKay, Inc., 1971.

Memories of a Great Lady

by Ardelia Dixon

Illustrated by Charlotte Durant

MEMORIES OF A GREAT LADY

by

Ardelia B. Dixon

"... A world I dream where black or white,
Whatever race you be,
Will share the.bounties of the earth
And every man is free.
Where wretchedness will hang its head,
And joy, like Pearl
Attends the needs of all mankind —
Of such I dream, my world!"

These lines were penned by one of the best known black poets and playwrights of our time, the late Langston Hughes. They were dedicated to the lady who is the subject of some wonderful memories, Miss Lottie Pearl Mitchell.

Langston Hughes, also author of *Fight for Freedom*, a history of the National Association for the Advancement of Colored People, tells of meeting Miss Mitchell at the tenth annual convention of the Association in Cleveland during World War I, about 1918. She impressed him then with her fiery pleas for racial equality, and for the next fifty-five years she continued her crusade for freedom. That is a long time to remain as actively involved in the struggle as this lady was. But whatever she believed, she believed with her whole being, and put everything she had into making it a reality.

Those of us who knew her well, and that number ran into the hundreds, probably the thousands, of the great and near-great, were hard put to decide which of the many causes she supported was the most important to her. Undoubtedly, the N.A.A.C.P. was very high on her list. She served on the National Board of Directors, as National Vice President, as well as being president of the local branch and holding numerous other offices. At one time, Miss Mitchell served the local branch as Executive Secretary without pay to prove one was needed. She won her point, and there has been a paid executive ever since. Miss Mitchell gave countless volunteer hours in persuading others to support the program. It was for good reason that she was known as "Miss N.A.A.C.P." throughout the country.

My own memories of Miss Mitchell go back to the time when she was advisor to the N.A.A.C.P. Youth Council of which I was a member. I was still in high school, and already she was a legend. Her name was synonymous with N.A.A.C.P. in Cleveland. There was no television to provide entertainment then, and people went to meetings or teas at the area churches on Sunday afternoons. The N.A.A.C.P. held frequent "mass meetings," as they were called, and always it was Miss L. Pearl Mitchell who made the appeal for funds, led the applause for the speaker of the day, and played the piano or directed the singing of "Lift Ev'ry Voice and Sing" which opened every meeting. The meetings were often spirited, the crowd enthusiastic, and it was in this way we youngsters learned much of Negro history and became acquainted with the infamous things that were going on in the South in the days preceding the civil rights legislation of the 1960's. Black leaders such as Thurgood Marshall, James Weldon Johnson, Mordecai Johnson, Judge William Hastie, became household words by being heard in these Sunday meetings. Always, Miss Mitchell was at the front of the church or on the platform, introducing the speaker or pleading for funds when he was through.

My friends and I were pleased when Miss Mitchell got some of us together and organized a Youth Council to the N.A.A.C.P. She served as its sponsor for several years, and it was during this time I grew to know her well, and respect her as a friend. She treated us like the sons and daughters she never had, schooled us in parliamentary procedure, helped us plan meaningful programs, and made us aware of how young people could assist in the fight for freedom. Yes, even then, in the mid-30's there were young people picketing, protesting, and demonstrating for causes. Miss Mitchell backed us all the way. We didn't call our tactics "nonviolence" then, but what was done, was done with dignity as

Miss Mitchell had taught us. We planned a splash party at the city-owned Garfield Park pool which was known to be segregated, and the pool was drained. On another occasion, we attempted to swim in the lake at the old Euclid Beach Park, another known discriminatory facility, and we were prevented from entering, by uniformed police. We went on the dance floor at the same park, and the band stopped playing. Several young whites joined us in these demonstrations, and they shared our respect for Miss Mitchell and her genteel militancy. She never taught hate — only that all were equal in the sight of God, and because of that, we should accept nothing less than equality in all phases of our lives. Separatism was foreign to her nature, and in the later years, she had trouble with the emphasis on "blackness." At a sorority regional conference in 1972, she protested, "If we are to remain an interracial organization, why can't we say simply *women* rather than *blacks?*" She was too busy "attending to the needs of all mankind to be bothered with polarization."

One of my last conversations with her before her final hospitalization was a telephone call. Her usual greeting, "Dedie, this is Pearl," was a bit weaker than usual, but alerted me that she was about to make one of her famous requests that one couldn't refuse. Then past the age of ninety, weakened by a series of illnesses, she was nevertheless continuing by telephone her life-long crusade for the support of the N.A.A.C.P. She extracted from me a promise I was duty-bound to keep, even when she had passed from the scene.

When the Ohio Conference of Branches was organized, Miss Mitchell was put in charge of youth work in the state. She was proud when several of her Cleveland young people were elected to office in the State Youth Council. She accompanied us on trips to meetings—our first real experience with conventions—and introduced us to the "big names" that we had heard from afar at the mass meetings—Walter White, Daisy Lampkin, Roy Wilkins, Juanita Jackson, and so many others. It was at our first national convention in Detroit in 1937 that Cleveland young people made

NAACP AKA AKA AKA AKA NAACP

Charlotte T. Durant

Lady Pearl Mitchell

friends with Gloster B. Current, now Director of Branches of the N.A.A.C.P., and other members of the Detroit Youth Council — encounters that were to ripen into lasting associations and friendships. Mr. Current was one who came from afar to pay a last tribute to Pearl when he heard of her passing.

Then there are my recollections of Miss Mitchell in connection with her beloved sorority — Alpha Kappa Alpha, the oldest black sorority in the country. This was another cause to which she was totally committed. I don't even remember actually discussing sorority with her, but it was her influence that guided some of us young civil righters to aspire to become part of her sisterhood. Simply because she belonged and was so devoted to its ideals, we knew that was the place for us. The fact that some of her former protégées should become her sorors filled her with pride.

In the sorority, I remember her insistence on correct procedure and ritual. Many times she would take the floor, even in the twilight of her life, to insist firmly on a point of order. She was usually right, and many of us were to say later that it was Pearl who "kept us on our toes." Likewise, her telephone calls or letters became fearsome or pleasant reminders of something we had done well or badly, as the case might be. Her standards were high, and she did not believe in compromise. For example, she was a purist about the name of the organization; with her, it had to be "Alpha Kappa Alpha," never A.K.A.

On the lighter side, she loved to dance, and was delighted when our escorts would ask her to dance at a sorority affair. And they always did. My favorite memory pictures of the dances were the times Miss Mitchell acceded to requests that she lead the singing of the sorority hymn. In the middle of that huge circle of beautifully-gowned women was this energetic, dimunitive lady, head held high, directing the singing of the sorority songs, in her own jaunty fashion — her face positively aglow.

I remember her also in the later years, when her health began to fail; her steps faltered a bit; her hearing was not as keen as formerly; but her spirit remained undaunted. She had several bouts with illness, and finally made the concession to use a cane as an aid to walking. But she came regularly to meetings, brought by a loyal soror, her mind still sharp, and her questions searching and pointed. Her last appearance at a sorority function was at the June fellowship luncheon, following a siege of illness. She appeared so weak, so frail, but with that sense of what was right and proper, she stood alone, unaided, and made her little speech. She thanked all the sorors for their kindness during her illness, and asked prayers that she would be able to attend the national meeting later in the summer.

She did not make that one; it was only the second time she had missed since she had joined the organization over fifty years before. And was she proud of that record! The other time had been because of illness, also. Indeed, poor health had plagued her for the greater portion of her life, and it was the more remarkable that she had been able to accomplish so much with so frail a body. One who did not know of her disabilities, however, could not have guessed. She was too busy doing what needed doing to complain about herself.

In the sorority, she was affectionately known as "Miss A.K.A." (Miss Alpha Kappa Alpha Sorority). She had been initiated into Zeta Chapter as an undergraduate at Wilberforce University, and it was immediately a love match between her and the sorority. During the years to follow, she was to hold practically every national office and become the third Supreme Basileus (national president) of the organization. Locally, she headed the chapter, and became Director of the Great Lakes Region. At regional conferences an award, named for her, is presented annually to the outstanding undergraduate chapter. It is fitting that this should be so, as undergraduates always related to her and she to them. She remained young at heart, and young people loved her as much in her latter years as had my contemporaries in her younger days. A soror said of her, "We alumnae may merit her concern and guidance, but her heart has always been with the undergrads ..."

I remember coming into a Sunday morning devotional

service at a regional conference a few years back to find her there before anyone, setting the tone of the inner serenity she had. Sorors fell silent to listen, tears welling up in many eyes. She was then in her late eighties. At another conference, when the call was made for all sorors who had ever sung in a chapter ensemble to participate with the current group, Pearl was one of the first to make her way up front.

I recall how touched she was when her local chapter had an appreciation luncheon in her honor a few years ago, and sorors and colleagues from all walks of life paid her tribute. She fairly beamed at the "Glimpses into Lady Pearl's Life" portion of the program. Two sorors related how she had helped solve a problem of discrimination for them on a college campus. One of her contemporaries, a retired school teacher, told of her intercession in a discriminatory matter in the school system in the early days when black teachers were still few in number. Young lawyers related her inspiration to them. Her minister told humorously how she kept him going, with full support, but also with reprimand when she deemed it necessary.

Incidentally, "Lady Pearl" was another of the nicknames that fit her so well. This was the one by which former Cleveland Mayor Carl B. Stokes addressed her. He was among a long list of influential persons who sought her counsel at any hour of the day or night. During his administration, Miss Mitchell was appointed to the Commission on the Aged, and was reappointed by his successor.

The third great interest in her life concerned her faith in God and her devotion to His church. For over fifty years, she was an active member of the Mt. Zion Congregational United Church of Christ. She directed the choir there for some fifteen years, and was at various times a trustee, a member of the building and finance committees, and once she served as executive secretary when the church was without a pastor. She was counselor and close friend to all the ministers, and was repaid by their constant devotion to her. A great comfort to her in her illness were the

49

frequent visits from her minister to the suburban convalescent home where she was confined. She confided to me haltingly how pleased she was that he visited her early on the morning he was to leave on a vacation trip. Neither of them realized it was to be their last meeting. He died suddenly shortly after his return, and she was too weak to be told.

How was it possible for one frail person to accommodate so much energy, so much drive, so much influence, that capacity to make such important contributions in so many areas and such an indelible impression on so many lives? Answers may be found in her early life experiences, many of which I learned in conversations with her. My big disappointment was that I was not able to persuade her to begin writing her own life story before her health failed. She had so much to say that is as relevant today as it was yesterday. Her life should be an inspiration to young people.

Her Christian faith and insistence on academic achievement she credited to her parents, both educators, who themselves made history at Wilberforce University. Her father, Dr. Samuel Mitchell, was an ordained Methodist minister, as well as an educator, who became president of Wilberforce. He had brought his family East from Jefferson City, Missouri, where he had headed Lincoln University. Their destination was Cleveland, but they stopped in Wilberforce to visit his wife's parents and his brother, John, one of the founders of historic Wilberforce University. They decided to remain there. Mrs. Mitchell was dean of several of the dormitories until her retirement, when she came to Cleveland to live with her daughter, Pearl.

Pearl, one of seven children, was born in Wilberforce and received her early education in the academic community there. She passionately loved music, played well by ear before taking formal training, and when only sixteen years of age, used her musical talents to accompany a group of African students who traveled about the country singing, earning money for their education. Pearl listened to their melodies, picked them up, and was able to accompany them. She often spoke of this experience as having an important impact on her life.

Later, she went to the Oberlin Conservatory of Music to pursue graduate study in music. But the desire to serve humanity prevailed, and she went to Kalamazoo College in Michigan for sociology courses, then to Hampton Institute, Virginia, for training in war camp community service. The latter training was to serve her well when she worked at Camp Dodge and Fort Des Moines during World War I.

Her father died at the age of 49; and as there were still three younger children to educate, Pearl joined her oldest brother, Charles, in Washington, where he was working as a messenger in the Library of Congress. Pearl obtained a typing job in the office of the Howard University Law School, remaining until the end of the war, when she moved to Cleveland for what was to be a long and fruitful stay. She attained first-place rating on a civil service examination and was appointed probation officer and investigator for the Juvenile Court, a position she was to fill with distinction until ill health forced her retirement after twenty years. However, her really active life was just beginning, and the post-retirement years were probably even more productive than the previous ones.

Besides her church work, there was the N.A.A.C.P., nationally and locally. She directed membership campaigns in several cities, her infectious enthusiasm causing membership rolls to skyrocket. She took on the life membership campaign as a personal challenge, enrolling family, friends, and associates, and leading her sorority to engage in a drive that brought in astronomical numbers of life memberships.

Somehow she found the time for other pursuits. She was gifted as an actress, was connected with the old Playhouse Settlement (forerunner of Karamu House), and as only a few persons remember, appeared in the first interracial play produced at the Cleveland Playhouse. The play was written by her friend, Jo Sinclair, an author native to Ohio.

I remember visiting Miss Mitchell in the large family home on East 95th Street — a formal, gracious place where pictures of

51

her family, especially her mother of whom she was very proud, were displayed, and some lovely old pieces of furniture stood. A beautifully-carved, heavy oak chest was her particular joy, and it went along when she moved to a smaller apartment in East Cleveland. The chest and her piano dominated that comfortable living room with its view of the entire city, a view which she proudly showed to visitors. She never lost her knack for conversation. One dropped by for a minute and usually stayed an hour, even in the latter days when the visitor was trying not to tire her. She was always a fascinating personality — thoughtful, grateful for little attentions, secure in the knowledge of who she was.

She and I worked to assemble her papers and memorabilia which had been requested by the Western Reserve Historical Society. We went together to deposit the material, and the curators of the Black Archives Project seemed to sense the greatness in her personality and explained in detail how the material would be catalogued and made available for reference. This was a proud moment for her. I got the feeling she was relieved at having insured the documentation of some of the things that had been important to her.

Awards and appointments came often to this great lady — from the N.A.A.C.P., from the sorority, from Wilberforce, from many national and local organizations. One that was very dear to her and about which she waxed eloquent frequently was her appointment to the Ohio Sailors' and Soldiers' Home Board by then Governor Frank J. Lausche. She was the only Negro and the only woman on the Board (long before the era of women's lib), and she served faithfully without pay for six years, making the semi-monthly trip by bus. She found segregation in the home set-up, and fought as only she could until it was abolished. Discrimination in any form, at whatever level, was an anathema to her. She died in 1974, still fighting for her dreams.

I remember her finally as a beautiful, uncompromising person—without peer—who took seriously her sorority's admonition to "serve all mankind." A high-principled lady, she had tremendous influence on all. I was privileged to have known her.

Bibliography

Hughes, Langston, *Fight for Freedom*. New York: W. W. Norton and Company, 1962.

Parker, Marjorie, *History of Alpha Kappa Alpha Sorority*, privately printed, 1966.

Turner, Marjorie, "Tribute to L. Pearl Mitchell," *The Crisis*. Dec., 1974, Vol. 81, No. 10, p. 349-351.

Much of the material for this account is based on private conversations with Ms. Mitchell.

Garrett Morgan
The Hidden Man

by David A. D. J. Wilson

Illustrated by Ron Smith

GARRETT MORGAN: THE HIDDEN MAN

by

David A. D. J. Wilson

The story of Garrett Morgan is for the most part unknown, especially among young blacks. It is truly regrettable that his is one which many black and white people never knew existed. Yet every time a pedestrian crosses the street, busy traffic stops on both sides, miraculously as it were, to allow him (or her) to pass. And all because of the safety light, which was Morgan's own conception. His creations and achievements have without a doubt reshaped our world, making it safer to live in, for he invented many lifesaving devices in the course of his own time. Garrett was also a chemist of sorts, concocting many useful aids for the hair grooming industry, up until that time an enterprise inaccessible to blacks.

Garrett Augustus Morgan was born in 1877, the son of a railroad worker and a preacher's daughter. His early life was tightly run, perhaps accounting for his generally stern, strict temperament. His father was a man who worked for everything. He didn't believe in the theory of "Taking Something for Nothing." This explains Garrett's business sense, for he was also taught that there was always a balance and nothing came easy. But above all other human qualities Elder Morgan loathed, there was one vice he would not tolerate: laziness.

Garrett and his family lived in the town of Claysville, Kentucky. The little town was named after Samuel Clay, a Civil War hero and the owner of many slaves.

There wasn't any public water system. There weren't any wells, either, so the populace of the tiny town had to walk nearly a mile into the courthouse in Paris to obtain the precious liquid that we take for granted at the turn of a faucet today. As a result of the water condition in Claysville, Morgan's father had the following to say in regards to laziness: "If the house were to catch fire, the water bucket would be the first thing to burn up." Garrett used that saying throughout his lifetime.

After a series of misadventures in his travels, young Garrett finally arrived in Cleveland in a freight car. The evening air was cool and gusty, refreshing against the dusty grey stateliness of the train station. The flaming sun burned the dusky sky, drawing forth from Garrett's memory other pleasant evenings spent much like this one, playing or, like now, thinking, in the grassy fields down home. The city seemed to possess an aura all its own, and it beckoned, "Garrett, Garrett," calling to him through the hiss and crashing of the white hot steam from the nostrils of the throbbing iron horse. In the horse of iron, he slept by night. By day he tramped through town as a stranger, inquiring fruitlessly about work. For three nights he dreamed strange dreams of smoke and death, of fame and huge coffers of wealth, undaunted, and soon after, he signed up for work as a janitor for the L. N. Gross Company, a sewing operation typical of the fruit of the American Industrial Revolution.

The L. N. Gross Company was housed in a large building set in concrete with thick grating across most of the windows. There were several rows of benches, and on those benches sat small, curious machines. They were driven by one of several gargantuan motors, located to the rear of the plant. And what curious machines they were! Garrett watched them with a deep fascination. He was observant of the way the gears, belts, clicking rods and the whirring flywheels all worked together, with a steady humming sound he knew was its heartbeat.

In a short time, Garrett proved himself worthy of a promotion—apprentice to the adjuster of the enormous and powerful engines that drove dozens of those newfangled sewing machines! It was truly a rare and fortunate occurrence that he should also find love and an everlasting companion in his wife-to-be, Maryanna, who was a sewing machine operator at the shop. At

58

L. N. Gross, he was allowed to carry his own calling cards, billing himself as an adjuster of power machines. He eventually became more experienced in business as a contractor for electrical work and gas-pipe fittings.

But while still employed in the sewing factory, he invented the Belt-Drive Fastener, an innovation that saved hours of repair time in the various shops all over the nation, and in time, the world over. As an apprentice to the adjuster, he noted that if the large belt connecting the motors to the machines broke, the man would have to place his hand into an auger, a huge needle with scissor-like holes for the fingers and thumb of the hand. The auger was used previously for repairing sails of canvas. The man would first have to take the auger and attempt to push it through the thick leather (for, you see, leather was used prior to the use of rubber from South America). Next, with something far short of surgical precision, he would lace the broken ends of the belt together with catgut, a thick, durable string. Sometimes this took an hour or more; it involved holding up workers by the dozens, and sometimes hundreds, at the employer's expense. In the factories during the Industrial Revolution, hundreds worked at times on just one special operation: mass production was the byword.

So in his leisure time, Garrett worked on the problem, coming up with a device that punched holes in the leather. He then put a zig-zagged strip of metal with pins for the holes onto the broken ends of the belt. Using yet another tool resembling pliers, he bound it together. The repaired area was now stronger than even the smooth, unbroken leather surface elsewhere on the belt. The entire operation took less than five minutes, expending less than ten times that of the method utilizing the auger approach. As a result of his timesaving invention, he became an overnight success, gaining much publicity for his discovery.

Once Garrett spent an evening working on a liquid polish for the stitching needles. It seemed that they were always scorching certain kinds of cloth in the process of stitching. He was almost onto the answer to this problem when a sudden call to dinner made him stop what he was doing. He hastily wiped the solution from his hands right onto a naturally soft and fuzzy pony fur cloth he used for polishing woods and metals. When he returned to his labors, he found the pony fur cloth no longer fuzzy and soft, but slick, shiny and very straight.

As was his habit, he slept on the incident with the usual pad and pen dangling above him on the headboard. This was done in the event that an idea should arrive by dream. Morning came with no notes scribbled on the pad, but there was an intent, rare and even humorous expression on the normally stern face. That could only mean one thing—Garrett was feeling childish, like when he would plot a ridiculous prank. And sure enough when his next-door neighbor let the family Airedale out to take its morning walk, just out of sight over there in the hedges was Garrett with a small jar of the stuff he'd used on that cloth the night before! Ah well, if the cloth didn't disappear overnight, then perhaps the dog wouldn't either. He quickly collared the Airedale and applied the pasty solution from the head to the wiry tail, making sure none got in the eyes. He let it go, which it did, running faster than the fleetest greyhound—across the lawn right back to its master's house. It was quite erect, whining and shivering, for the protective crew-cut style fur that was its pride in fighting was no longer that way. Anyone just guessing what had happened to his dog would have assumed that it might have taken an early morning swim. And much to Garrett's humor, the canine's irate master, upon expecting his favorite pet, found to his dismay a worthless, miserable (and soon homeless) mutt. He kicked the poor animal off his porch, chasing after it a few steps and calling after it with the most abusive language.

One house up and safely inside, Garrett chuckled at the scene. But a fire welled up in his eyes, replacing the mischievous sparkle there only a moment before. If this man couldn't even recognize his own pet Airedale, what a difference it might make on one's profile—on a black person at that! He gave the matter ample and serious thought. Shortly after, he made plans to become an entrepreneur in the market of—what else but—hair grooming and processing. So not long after this decision, he departed from the L. N. Gross Company amid much regret from both sides. Later he would wed Maryanna and begin his business, which was the first of its kind. The G. A. Morgan Hair Refining Company produced hair straightener for men, G. A. Morgan's Italian Hair Oil, and even a harmless dye that put a pleasant stain in the hair of the user. The business boomed, as Garrett built up a steadily growing line of black clientele. He kept his business running, and in 1913 turned his attentions to other areas of import, primarily in the line of personal safety equipment which later was produced on behalf of the national interest.

The year was 1913. Morgan had been experimenting with a totally original safety device. Soon afterward, he was invited to attend the International Exposition of Safety and Sanitation at the Grand Central Palace in New York City. It was a gala celebration. Naturally he represented the United States, while others hailed from different parts of Europe: France, England, Belgium, Germany and The Netherlands. In the hush of silence and the tension that followed the demonstrations of each country's product, Garrett, much to his own astonishment as well as that of the others, received his First Grand Prize for his "Morgan Safety Hood Device." Now suddenly surrounded by cheers and waves of applause, he was also presented with a quarter-pound of solid gold for his achievement. The caption on the First Grand Prize read: "Let us preserve life," which was indeed his own motto.

Shortly after the brilliant demonstration at the safety exhibition, he formed his own safety business, the Morgan National Safety Device Company. Victor W. Sincere of the Bailey Company and Newton D. Baker, a renowned philanthropist, were among those on the Board of Directors.

Garrett began selling stocks to blacks at ten dollars a share. Although that phase of the business was open exclusively to blacks, none would invest. The second year it cost fifty dollars a share, and the third time around, just to do business in the lower lobby, one had to pay from eighty to one-hundred dollars for one share of Morgan Safety Stock. Among other things of good fortune, the American La France Fire Engine Company of Elmira, New York decided to collaborate by merger and get on the bandwagon. They received Morgan's permission and today the Elmira based firm is the single largest fire safety company in the world.

Many things happened for Garrett Morgan and the world in 1914. War was one of them. For him it was truly a blessing in disguise. Canada, our northern neighbor, entered early. Recalling the Safety Expo of the year before, Canadian officials asked Morgan for more information on his hood and, if possible, an actual demonstration of its application. The mask Morgan designed was undoubtedly useful; however, the two long-breathing hoses at the bottom of the hooded facepiece made it difficult for soldiers to move swiftly. It was also awkward to carry. Thus, it was necessary to modify the mask. The hood was made more compact, and less heavy; the hoses were shortened and the charcoal cylinders inside them were made thicker. With these modifications, the forces of Canada moved for more of Morgan's devices to be installed in the cigar-shaped submarines that prowled the dark depths of enemy oceans. They were also widely employed on the battlefield where the Germans were engaged in chemical warfare. Yellow shrouds of chlorine gas caused the eyes to water from the intense burning it caused in them; a gagging sensation in the entire respiratory system sent a man retching. Without much warning, the deadly clouds would roll silently down a bomb-torn hillside to the unknowing soldiers below. But they were safe, thanks to Garrett Morgan's improvised safety hood, now known as the gas mask.

England also joined the war early and the United States became involved in the power struggle against Germany in 1917. All of these countries had every one of their soldiers on the field using Morgan's breathing apparatus, now modified so that the troops could pack them into their sacks. Thus Garrett Morgan was a silent hero who had a key part in the safety of our soldiers in the war. There was also another time he was a hero—and this time a more involved one. The incident was at Crib Number Five, Cleveland City Waterworks, in 1916.

On the evening of July 24th at ten o'clock, a tremendous explosion shook the ground from below. Licking orange flames and billowing cotton smoke rose up mingling with the navy sky. More than two-hundred and fifty feet below the surface of Lake Erie, either a flint having been struck or a spark from a vein of metal exposed by a tired worker's pickax caused an invisible gas to come to life, leaving all in its wake dead from fumes or flames. Rescue parties were hurriedly set up by the nervous workers and sent down the roughly-hewn air shaft, never to return to clean, cool night air again. Thrice they went down, three times they failed. But someone recalled a man named Morgan and his safety helmets. In a frenzy the Marine Officer was contacted. The City Detective arrived on the scene and, along with the Manager of the City, he was asked to call Mr. Morgan.

Garrett Morgan received all three calls within five minutes' time at three in the morning. Wide awake and alert, he left without hat, coat or shirt against the wishes of his wife Maryanna. He didn't even throw on a pair of shoes! He quickly called his brother Frank who lived next door. They packed more than two-dozen of the hoods in Garrett's automobile and flew off into the night. The car screeched around quiet street corners with the two brothers speaking urgently to one another. The twenty-five masks looked like a tangled octopus catch on the back seat.

The Police Captain and Mayor Davis were awaiting them on the Ninth Street Pier; from there, with the bizarre safety hoods, they rode across the high swell of the sea in a belabored tugboat, the *George C. Wallace*. Once on Whiskey Island, a tiny smudge of land in the sea just a little way from the Flats, they raced to the scene, guided by the curious and excited mob. Garrett immediately asked for volunteers but only got sullen stares, fear, and silent apathy mingled with the dissonant calls of liners, tugs and freighters wailing in the early morning. Frank wasn't going to let his brother go down there alone. Anything that should happen would happen to both of them. Thomas Clancy, whose father seemed to be missing from the ranks of those helplessly above this chaotic inferno that raged below, joined the determined duo. He had a gnawing feeling that his father was down there, somewhere. The Mayor took Morgan's hand in his, sadly bidding these three brave men farewell, as though for the last time. They then entered the iron boxcar to descend the smoking shaft.

The fumes wrapped tightly about the rescuers like a misty, velvet shroud. The car hit the ground with a muffled clang, and the men stumbled out, grovelling like a trio of grotesque Minotaurs in the catacombs of the miner's forsaken world. Somewhere down in one of the passages, Garrett's foot bumped against something that was firm like an inert body. He bent down and like a blind man sought to find the wrist of the miner. Checking for a pulse he found the wrist limp and lifeless. But in the dead man's hand was a flashlight. It was like another world, in another place, another time in this eternity of a subterranean silence—but wait! A groan. It came from over there! The body seemed to be lifeless, but there seemed a chance yet of it being alive. Thomas Clancy couldn't make the features out in all this smoke, yet he felt it was someone who was very close to him. They loaded the man into one of the mining rail-cars to safety. When they came out of the iron box, like a school of frightened fish, the crowd jumped back in one movement. Could it be that these were monsters of the deep earth, unleashed from some nameless place by the explosion? But reasoning returned when the workers saw them bringing the semblance of a miner from the boxcar and gently placing him on a pile of soft dirt. A team of doctors brought blankets as the policemen brushed aside the men staring curiously at the one on the ground. He turned and writhed in intense pain and agony, still fighting the death rattle that shook him with the vestiges of a fading, ebbing strength; he would live, though. Through the contorted features of the face, it could be seen that this was Mister

Van Dusen, the superintendent of the operation. Thomas Clancy's nagging suspicions had been right, for much to his joy he was reunited here above ground with his father.

At once the mob moved as one large body toward the pile of masks, and it seemed that everyone wanted to get into the act. After many gruesome and anxious hours eleven men were collected alive! However, only two survived. But still it proved to the City that Morgan's device could protect one against the ravages of smoking death. Garrett didn't end his work of inventing life-saving devices with his safety hood, though. In another instance, Garrett Morgan was witness to a horse and auto accident. A little girl was hurt and this particular experience was one that deeply touched the tender spot in Morgan's heart. He set about building a contrivance that would control the traffic speeding through the intersections. When a lever was raised, it caused a red signal to light up. A sign which read "stop" would also at the same time drop down from a slot on the side of the box. The stop sign was horizontal and easily seen by both pedestrians and drivers.

The first working model was used to demonstrate the ease and the efficiency with which the traffic light directed and controlled traffic. It was installed at an intersection in Willoughby, Ohio. The next was temporary and was put out on 105th Street, East. A third, more permanent light was hooked up at Ninth and Euclid Avenue. The product was practical and became widespread. Today it is no longer a rectangular, white box, for it has since been improved. It is even more streamlined and yellow, with goggle-like covers over the apertures to cut glare. The red "stop," yellow "caution," and green "go" signs are there and, as they were then, still working together to save lives.

One day Garrett received news of a person dying in a bedroom fire. Like so many other times, the cause was a cigarette that hadn't been put out before the victim dozed off. For the problem at hand, Garrett, now besieged with declining health, old age and the painful semi-blindness of glaucoma, created a water pellet that could be placed in the cigarette up next to the filter.

Thus, until the advent of nonflammable materials being put into pillows, cushions and mattresses, many lives were spared by the ingenious invention.

Though Garrett Morgan never entertained the thought of death, it came to his bedside on July 26th in 1963. During his life, there was a testimonial given at City Hall at which a trusted friend and associate, Justice Harold Burton, made a brief, yet everlasting, speech in which he said: "By his deeds he shall be remembered." In the face of adversity and racial prejudice Garrett Morgan stood quite tall. He truly was and still is someone well worth remembering.

All biographical information given through courtesy of The Garrett Morgan Files of the Black History Archives, property of the Western Reserve Historical Society. Also, certain parts of this article were obtained in a private phone conversation with Garrett Morgan, Jr.

Zelma

by Ebraska D. Ceasor

Illustrated by Ron Smith

ZELMA

by

Ebraska D. Ceasor

"And how was your day, Zelma?" her father asked. He was smiling, but Zelma wasn't sure he would approve of her spending most of the day singing and playing the piano. She hesitated, looking at her mother for support.

"Oh, Zelma has been wonderful," her mother said softly. "She's been helping me teach the little ones some new songs."

Zelma stopped squirming as she continued to eat her dinner, grateful for her understanding mother.

The evening meal in the Watson household had become a kind of ritual. The parents set high standards for their six children and all had to give an account of how they had spent each day. The Reverend Samuel Watson was a kind man, deeply religious, and blessed with wisdom far beyond his years. Even though he was a strict father, he was loving and proud of his children.

"Maybe I can't brag about my ancestors," he often said, "but I am an ancestor! Look at my children."

Lena Watson, the mother, was a beautiful person spiritually and physically. She ran a well-organized household.

Zelma's parents had met at Bishop College in Dallas, Texas, in 1895 and married after a seven-year engagement. They were now settled in Dallas. He was pastor of a large and influential church. It was not unusual to see Black leaders like Booker T. Washington, W. E. B. DuBois, James Weldon Johnson, and A. Phillip Randolph discussing, debating, expounding their philosophies in the Watson living room.

Zelma was enthralled as she sat quietly at her father's feet listening to "the great ones" talk. She was thankful that she was the eldest and was not carted off to bed like the other children

71

when this exciting talk was going on.

The Watson household was full of children's laughter, young voices singing, many feet running and playing. Religion and education were important to the parents. They saw to it that their children received a rich abundance of both. Mrs. Watson had been a schoolteacher before she married. She and her husband taught their children at home. They were not satisfied with the quality of education provided for Afro-Americans in the places where they lived.

Sometimes the children studied outside on the grass, using stones for desks. The mothers packed picnic lunches and brought them out to the children. Sometimes the children caught their lunches in the streams. Crawfish tasted mighty good, freshly caught and cooked outside.

Rev. Watson was as concerned about his congregation and his neighbors as he was about his children. He often visited the jails, talking to prisoners, many of them unjustly accused. When he was convinced of a prisoner's innocence, he helped raise funds for his legal defense.

Because he befriended one such prisoner, Rev. Watson was warned to leave town in forty-eight hours. Knowing his love for his eldest daughter, the Ku Klux Klan had threatened to kill Zelma if her father did not reveal certain information. Zelma still has haunting nightmares of this frightening ordeal.

"We'll go to Topeka!" Rev. Watson shouted as his eyes fell upon a letter on his desk which had come a few days before, offering him a pastorate in Topeka, Kansas. When he had received the letter, he had laid it aside not sure how to answer it. Without delay, the family started to pack the few things they would take with them. Topeka offered new freedoms. The church, with a beautiful parsonage next door, was located in a section called "Free Town." During the Civil War, this section of the city had been settled by escaped slaves, freed men, men who had never been enslaved, and others who were seeking a new and better life. Topeka had only one high school. Here, the fourteen-year-old

Zelma had her first experience of going to school with white children. She met the competition successfully. She was a good student with a beautiful voice and a friendly, engaging smile.

One day Zelma came home in tears. "Of, Father, something terrible happened in school today!" she cried, rushing into her father's comforting arms. "They called me 'Fatty' and they laughed at me. What am I going to do?" she sobbed.

Zelma had always been large for her age, but it never seemed to matter before. Now, because her peers had begun to giggle and make fun of her, she was sensitive and embarrassed.

"The only thing that will stop them is to excel in some visible way," her father said. "We'll teach you to skate, play tennis, volleyball, and basketball. You will learn to do things that people think big girls can't do. You will learn to do them better than anybody. So dry your eyes, my dear; we have work to do."

Zelma and her father set up an intensive training program—he coaching, advising, teaching; she, practicing, learning, and excelling. The giggles and teasing didn't stop altogether; however, Zelma was better able to live with the fact that she was and would always be heavy and of large stature.

One day, during her senior year in high school, Zelma walked into her father's study and announced, beaming, "I'm going to the University of Chicago." Her father offered no objection.

Zelma eagerly set about preparing her application forms. Days passed. Finally, the letter that she had so anxiously awaited came. She tore it open with trembling fingers and read, "Dear Miss Watson, your credentials are all in order. We are pleased to enroll you in the freshman class of the University of Chicago. Please report to the Admissions Office on October 3, 1920. However, we do not have any rooms left in the dormitory you have chosen or in any on campus. Do you have friends in the city with whom you can arrange lodging? ... " Zelma bit her lip as she read, trying desperately to hold back the tears.

Rev. Watson comforted her. "Don't worry, Zelma. I'll think of something. You will go to the University of Chicago. But you

73

can't live in Chicago alone!"

In a few weeks an answer to his many letters came. The Pilgrim Baptist Church in Chicago was seeking a new pastor. They would be pleased if the Reverend Samuel Watson would accept the position. Jubilation filled the Watson household. The children were excited. They were moving to Chicago!

Rev. Watson drove around Chicago, pointing out to his family things of interest—the beautiful lake, the Art Institute, the tall buildings, the Pilgrim Baptist Church. He saved the first look at their new home for last. At last, he drove up to a large three-story house with heavy oaken doors and leaded windows on Chicago's South Side at 36th and Vincennes Avenue. Inside, the house was charming, the most beautiful place the Watsons had ever owned.

College life for Zelma was full of rich and rewarding experiences. Oftentimes, she and her father would study together in the University library. How she treasured those hours! She felt his equal as they sat over the many books and learned together. At last she felt that he approved of her. She felt that she had even succeeded in erasing his early disappointment: she was not the son whom he had hoped, expected and even prayed his first-born would be. She knew he was proud of her many achievements.

Zelma graduated from the University of Chicago in 1924 with a Ph.B. degree in Sociology. She had been a member of the Women's Athletic Association, the Alpha Kappa Alpha Sorority, president of the Inter-Collegiate Club, and had helped establish the first integrated YWCA in the country. Zelma studied organ at Northwestern University and voice at the American Conservatory of Music in Chicago.

Samuel E. J. Watson died suddenly in 1925 at forty-seven years of age. Though grief-stricken and now without the wisdom, counsel, and affection of this great man, Zelma and her mother resolutely set about the task of raising and educating the younger members of the family. Mrs. Watson became Dean of Women at Virginia Union University in Richmond and later was Coordinator

74

of Religious Activities at Tennessee A. and I. State University. She was honored in 1957 with the dedication of the Lena T. Watson Center for Freshmen at the University. All of her six children and their families attended the ceremony.

Zelma worked as a social caseworker, a probation officer, and in 1932, accepted a position of Dean of Women and Director of Personnel Administration at Tennessee A. and I. State University. In the meantime, she and her mother completed their family task. The younger children were now all college graduates: Verta, a chemist; young Samuel, a minister; Vivian, Director of Youth Programs in her husband's church; Cathryn, Elementary School Principal; and Jewel, Actuary and Secondary Teacher.

In 1969, Zelma received the Alumni Citation of the University of Chicago Alumni Association. In her acceptance speech to the Association, after telling of the rich experiences she had there, Zelma commended them upon their growth. She cited several incidents that were a blight upon the four years she spent at the University of Chicago. First she told of her exclusion from dormitory life and the college choir because of her race.

"Oh, your voice is much too good to be included in our choir. Your presence in the choir would be as disturbing to the worship atmosphere as the limp of a lame person in a procession," the choir master told her.

Zelma also recalled her first day in the swimming pool. She explained why she affectionately calls her right knee her "interracial knee." It had been injured in a basketball incident and corrective gymnastics led her to the swimming pool. When Zelma arrived for her swimming class, she handed the teacher her class card, and was told, as were the others, to get into the shallow end, play around a bit, and get used to the water. Zelma stepped into the pool; all the others climbed out as if they had been washed ashore. Zelma continued to paddle around alone in the pool, the girls staring at her in silence.

"I'm not accustomed to swimming with niggers!" one young lady said boldly to the teacher.

Looking the girl straight in the eye, the teacher replied quietly, "It's quite all right, my dear. Swimming is an elective. You are free to discontinue at any time." Then she continued to check the class cards. Slowly the others returned to the pool, while the indignant young lady stalked out.

Zelma commended the University for the integrity and expertise of this faculty member.

Zelma continued her climb upward. She founded and directed The Avalon Community Center in Los Angeles, California. While in California, she began a comprehensive study of Black music. She received a grant for such a study from the Rockefeller Foundation in 1942. This brought her to Cleveland, Ohio, so she could use the Cleveland Library's John G. White Collection, famous for its material on Afro-Americans.

"Now, Zelma, I have a nice gentleman who will escort you to the party Friday night. Please say you'll go."

"Okay, I'll go," she said without any hesitation. Zelma hung up the phone. She had only been in Cleveland a few days. Her Alpha Kappa Alpha Sorority sisters were making sure she would meet people and become involved in community activities. They wanted to be sure she would enjoy herself at the party and selected her escort carefully.

When Attorney Clayborne George, Chairman of the Civil Service Commission, called for her, Zelma was impressed by his quiet dignity. A recent widower, he was a gentleman and a scholar. She had a wonderful time and they became great friends.

In the meantime, Zelma continued her studies, which sometimes took her out of the city. She received a M.A. degree in Personnel Administration from New York University in 1943 and also continued research on her doctorate. Mr. George communicated with her every day that she was away with cards, flowers, letters, phone calls, and telegrams. Two years after they met, they were married.

During the next ten years, Zelma became very involved in the Cleveland activities. The Georges hosted many parties and functions in their home on East 81st Street. They were not merely social gatherings, however. Always they were meaningful occasions —a person of some importance in the educational, cultural, or political world would be present; or some important issue was discussed and resolved. The Georges made a handsome couple, complementing each other. She was warm, radiant, and exuberant; he was quieter, more reserved, a perfect gentleman.

Mr. George encouraged her in all she did. It was at his insistence and expense that she completed work on her doctorate. She received a Ph.D. in Sociology-Inter Cultural Relations from New York University in 1954. In 1959, Zelma went on a six-month lecture tour around the world as a "private citizen on a grant from the United States Department of State." She only consented to go on the world tour if Mr. George would join her later. He promised to meet her in Italy since he didn't want to go to the tropics. Her letters to him told how much she missed him and of her anxiety to see him in Italy. Always, he made excuses as to when he would join her. After the first four or five months had passed and he hadn't joined her, she began to suspect the truth. When she returned home, he confessed that he never intended to join her, that he knew she would not have gone otherwise.

This was typical of their relationship. He understood her need to extend herself, realizing he was what he termed "a home-body." Once, when Zelma came home after being away several weeks, Mr. George gave her several pretty house dresses for Christmas, gently hinting that he enjoyed having her at home—though never standing in her way if she had commitments away from home. The Georges had a way of being close together even when they were physically apart.

Clayborne George was a person of stature, highly respected in the community. In 1960, Antioch Baptist Church honored him at a testimonial dinner. His friends and colleagues praised him in speech after speech with sincerity and affection.

Clayborne George died on Christmas Eve, 1970, after a long illness. He was eighty-two years old. Zelma recalls their last day together, not as one of mourning and despair, but as one of reminiscing and thankfulness for the rich, full, and beautiful life they had shared.

Recently, when speaking of her husband, Dr. George said, "Among the myriad of beautiful things Cleveland has given to me, the best was Clayborne. He glorified and sweetened every day of my life, surrounded me with his strength, his tenderness, and his goodness."

Dr. George's other accomplishments and achievements are many and varied. To name a few: she was appointed by President Eisenhower in 1960 to the United States Delegation to the fifteenth General Assembly of the United Nations; Honorary membership in numerous fraternal organizations; Alumnus of the Year Awards from New York University and the University of Chicago; the Dahlberg Peace Award; the Distinguished Daughter of Ohio Award; honorary doctorates from Cleveland State University, Baldwin-Wallace and Heidelberg Colleges; and the Ursula Laurus Medal from Ursuline College, which is not given every year and considered to be more important than an honorary doctorate. In November, 1974, after having served for eight years, Dr. George retired as Director of the Cleveland Job Corps for Women. Dr. George was also a judge in the Miss America Contest in 1969. She jokingly refers to this event by recalling that she was the "only size 46 judge they have ever had."

She was also an opera singer. She sang the title role in *The Medium* at Karamu Theatre in Cleveland, and later on Broadway for thirteen weeks, which won for her the Merit Award of the National Association of Negro Musicians. She also distinguished herself in Menotti's *The Consul* at Cleveland's Play House and in *The Three Penny Opera* at Karamu.

Zelma has done extensive research and is a writer of note. From her pen have come: "Negro Music in American Life," a chapter in *The American Negro Reference Book*, edited by John P. Davis; an *Annotated Bibliography of Negro Folk Music*, and *Art Music by Negro Composers Based on Negro Thematic*

Material, a card file of 12,163 titles of music and literature; and *The Social Conditions of Slavery as Found in Slave Narratives*, an unpublished manuscript. She is currently working on an autobiography.

Dr. George says she knows who she is and where she wants to go, calling herself a "member of the commonwealth of man." She sums up her philosophy of life by saying that she looks forward to the day when we don't have to be Black or white, only human beings. We need to know more about other peoples, other cultures. The important concept we have to deal with is the "individual ... the infinite uniqueness, the dignity and worth of the <u>one</u>."

Bibliography

February, 1975, Biographical Sketch, *Clayborne and Zelma George,* file of newspaper clippings. Cleveland Public Library, Reference Department.

Jelliffe, Rowena Woodham, *Here's Zelma.* Cleveland, Ohio, October, 1971.

Keegan, Frank L., *Blacktown, U.S.A.,* Little, Brown, and Co., Boston, 1971.

Personal knowledge and interviews by the writer.